STRAIGHT TALKING ABOUT DRUGS

Cannabis

Sean Connolly

FRANKLIN WATTS
LONDON•SYDNEY

An Appleseed Editions book

First published in 2006 by Franklin Watts
338 Euston Road, London NW1 3BH

Franklin Watts Australia
Hachette Children's Books
Level 17/207 Kent St, Sydney, NSW 2000

© 2006 Appleseed Editions

Created by Appleseed Editions Ltd,
Well House, Friars Hill, Guestling,
East Sussex TN35 4ET

Designed by Guy Callaby
Edited by Pip Morgan
Artwork by Karen Donnelly
Picture research by Cathy Tatge

ISBN 0 7496 6757 5

Dewey Classification: 362.29' 5

A CIP catalogue for this book is available from
the British Library.

Photograph acknowledgements
Photographs by Alamy (Edward Parker), Guy Callaby, Getty Images
(Michael L. Abramson / Time Life Pictures, Daniel Arsenault, Neil
Beckerman, Per-Eric Berglund, Bruno Press, Peter Cade, Matt Cardy,
Christopher Bissel, Bill Crump, Marco Di Lauro, JAY DIRECTO / AFP,
Julia Fullerton-Batten, RAMZI HAIDAR / AFP, Jo Hale, Sandy Huffaker,
Hulton Archive, Maike Jessen, Erica Lansner, Ron Levine, Don
MacKinnon, Mario Magnani / Liaison, Mansell / Time Life Pictures,
Greg Marinovich, Doug Menuez, Gilles Mingasson / Liaison, Natalie
Pecht, ADALBERTO ROQUE / AFP, Rosebud Pictures, Fredrik Skold,
Simon Songhurst, Sion Touhig, Donald Weber, Ron Wurzer)

Printed in China

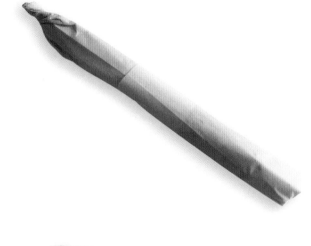

Contents

Have you ever been fed up or worried and felt like putting your cares aside for a while? Or maybe you and your friends noticed something funny together and shared a moment of laughter. Cannabis is a drug that seems to give people these relaxed and happy times. It certainly changes the way people see and feel things.

Cannabis, or marijuana, is the most common illegal drug in the world. Millions of people of all ages smoke it regularly and most began taking it when they were young. Have you ever been at a party where you saw people passing a cigarette between them, each inhaling a lungful of smoke that had a distinctive smell? Perhaps you have even been offered one of these joints and were tempted to say yes. This book will help you understand what cannabis is, what it can do to you, who takes it and why.

These unusual sunglasses show the distinctive leaves of the cannabis plant.

A little boost

People often turn to substances to help them to relax, cover up their worries or prolong their pleasure. Many adults drink alcohol as a way of loosening up or giving themselves a little boost. Other people prefer to smoke cannabis because they find that this makes boring things seem a little more bearable, and even funny.

A lot of people have come to believe that taking cannabis is a safer way of relaxing than drinking alcohol. Some actually grow it themselves. In the UK about 60 per cent of the cannabis smoked is grown at home and not brought in from other countries. People sell and trade seeds for types of cannabis such as skunk, which can be up to 10 times more powerful than traditional cannabis.

A hidden price

You may have heard the saying "there's no such thing as a free lunch". It means that there is usually a hidden price to pay for something that seems – at first – to be good. It would be great fun to be able to switch on a good mood whenever you want to, and keep it on for a few hours. But cannabis changes the way the brain works, although it is unclear how damaging this change might be – even after many years of research. Some scientists fear that, by smoking cannabis regularly, people risk permanent damage to their memory.

Another big concern is that cannabis can make you feel bad. Some people try cannabis once and feel frightened and disturbed, so vow never to try it again. Others might take it when their brain is already struggling to overcome depression or schizophrenia; for them the cannabis experience could be very frightening.

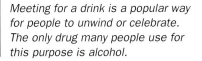

Meeting for a drink is a popular way for people to unwind or celebrate. The only drug many people use for this purpose is alcohol.

SEARCHING QUESTION

Cannabis is sometimes sold and even smoked near schools and playgrounds. Would you recognize what was happening if you saw people smoking it? Would you be able to tell whether a person was smoking cannabis or an ordinary cigarette?

Cannabis plants sprouting buds in the wild. If they have enough sunshine and water, cannabis plants can reach a height of 6 metres.

HOW CANNABIS IS SOLD

Cannabis leaves are dried and sold in clear bags. Dried buds, which contain more THC than the leaves, are sometimes mixed in. The bags are sold by weight: in the UK, an ounce (28 gram) bag is usually the largest, while smaller bags weigh half an ounce, a quarter of an ounce and so on. Dealers in Australia and other countries sell it in multiples of grams. In 2005, UK cannabis users paid about £70 for a one-ounce bag, while in Australia, a one-gram bag of cannabis cost A$15–25.

The word cannabis comes from *Cannabis sativa*, the scientific name for a plant that grows naturally in many parts of the world. There is nothing very unusual about the appearance of this plant, apart from its narrow, serrated leaves, which you may have seen on the front of some T-shirts. For many years, the plant has been a source of tough fibres (known as hemp), which are used to make rope, twine and textiles.

The leaves and buds of the cannabis plant are most important for those who smoke cannabis because of the chemicals they contain. The chief active ingredient is delta-9 tetrahydrocannabinol (THC for short), which is a drug that can change a person's mood. Once THC enters the brain, it creates changes in the way people behave and experience things. These are known as getting high.

A long history

People have known about the properties of cannabis for more than 4,000 years. According to historical evidence, cannabis was used as a medicine in India, China and parts of the Middle East. Chinese doctors treated malaria, rheumatism and other illnesses with cannabis. Elsewhere, it was used to dull people's aches and pains.

Europeans first learned of its painkilling properties in the late Middle Ages from traders who travelled from the Middle East and Asia. People drank the cannabis in the form of a tincture, but did not usually smoke it. By the 19th century, such cannabis preparations were sold legally in many countries. In England, Queen Victoria's doctor even recommended it to her to reduce the pain of menstrual cramps (period pains).

By the end of the 1800s, cannabis fell from favour as a medicine – partly because other painkillers, such as aspirin, were introduced. However, people had discovered the drug's other properties – it seemed to create feelings of pleasure and made people feel good. A new chapter in cannabis use was about to begin.

 When pure and administered carefully, [cannabis is] one of the of the most valuable medicines we possess. 〃

Queen Victoria's personal physician, Sir Russell Reynolds, describing cannabis in the first issue of the British medical journal *The Lancet* (1890).

These Vietnamese women display fabrics made with hemp fibres and dyed with indigo.

Naga Babas, Hindu holy men, smoke hashish regularly and especially during rites at the Kumbh Mela Festival every year. They are followers of the Hindu god Shiva, who is considered to be the god of hashish.

How people take cannabis

Most cannabis users smoke a mixture of dried leaves and flowers. They crumble the mixture into a cigarette paper and roll it into a home-made cigarette, known as a joint. They may mix the cannabis with tobacco to make the joint burn more smoothly, or smoke the leaf–flower mixture in pipes called chillums or water pipes (bongs). They inhale the smoke deeply and hold it in their lungs for a few seconds – the THC enters the bloodstream quickly and soon reaches the brain.

Cannabis resin is also smoked. When it is removed from the plant the resin is like the sap of an evergreen tree. As it hardens it is formed into sticky balls, firmer blocks or flakes, which vary in colour from light brown to deep black. This is known as hashish. It can also be made by compressing the pollen from the flowers.

Some hashish contains higher amounts of THC than the leaves and flowers, so the effects of smoking it may be greater. However, a few powerful strains of cannabis leaf can match the THC levels of hashish. Hashish can be made stronger still by boiling it in certain chemicals to produce a liquid known as hash oil. This oil can contain up to 25 times more THC than cannabis leaves.

Leaves, buds, hashish and hash oil can also be cooked and eaten. One way is to add the cannabis to a cake or biscuit mixture. Cannabis in biscuits and cakes such as brownies takes longer to have an effect, as the THC is only released once the food is digested. This delay can carry a risk – people might think they hadn't used enough cannabis and eat more, and so have a bad experience when the drug finally reaches the brain.

DEADLY HASHISH

Today the word assassin describes someone who murders an important person for religious or political reasons. The word originally referred to a member of a religious group in the Middle East. From the 11th to the 13th century, these extremists would swoop down from their mountain hide-outs to murder their religious rivals. Before setting out on their raids, they took hashish to develop visions of paradise (which they believed would be their reward). This habit led to the name they were given by other Arabs – hashshashun, meaning 'hashish smokers'.

←

A shopkeeper displays bongs (water pipes) and other products related to cannabis smoking.

A growing trade

↑ *Charles Baudelaire, the famous 19th-century French poet, drew this self-portrait under the influence of hashish.*

No-one knows how many people used cannabis for pleasure in the 19th century. Some famous people readily talked about their experiences. In the early 1800s, some English poets and writers admitted to using opium, a stronger drug that leads to dream-filled sleep.

By the middle of the century, hashish had become popular with French artists and writers. In the 1850s, some of them formed the hashish users' club.

Feeling rebellious

During the 20th century, cannabis became a drug used by millions of people around the world. By the 1930s, most countries had made it illegal, but this didn't stop people from smoking it. As a result, it became the most widely used illegal drug in the world.

The rise in use mirrored some changes in society, especially after the Second World War when the US, and to a lesser extent some other Western countries, became very wealthy.

Advertisements persuaded people their lives would be better and they would be happier if they bought the products that this new wealth was able to manufacture. These included TVs, dishwashers, refrigerators, second cars and bigger houses. People were encouraged to keep up with their neighbours and compete in a sort of race to buy the newest and biggest products.

Dropping out

Other people, including popular writers such as Jack Kerouac, believed this rat race was foolish. For them, happiness came from new experiences rather than buying more things.

By the 1960s, many young people were following the advice of Harvard University psychologist Timothy Leary, who urged them to "tune in, turn on and drop out" of what he saw as society's boring old ways of thinking. However, most people were afraid to take LSD, the powerful drug favoured by Leary. They turned to cannabis when they felt rebellious instead. Young people followed the example of many pop stars, who smoked cannabis and took other drugs.

FACT

Cannabis is California's largest cash crop. Officials estimate that it is worth $3–5 billion (£1.7–2.8 billion) each year. Compare this amount with the leading legally produced crops: grapes ($2.6 billion), lettuce ($1.4 billion) and flowers ($1 billion).

During the Roaring Twenties, a decade when alcohol was outlawed in the US, many jazz musicians smoked cannabis instead.

DIY drugs

Cannabis has become even more popular since the 1960s, and some of the people who first smoked it as teenagers are still using it as they near retirement. Most people still consider it to be safer than other illegal drugs (and in some people's view, safer than alcohol). Another reason for its popularity is that, unlike ecstasy or cocaine, cannabis is seen as natural – it is not produced in a laboratory.

Much of the cannabis smoked around the world is home-grown, either in secret locations out of doors or inside people's homes. Most of this cannabis is used by the growers. This makes it hard for the police to control the use of the drug as they would, for example, cocaine or heroin (where supplies can be reduced by a successful police raid on dealers).

Cannabis growers trade information about growing techniques as they develop and grow new strains. In addition, they buy and sell the seeds of successful new strains. Although this buying and selling is just as illegal as buying and selling cannabis leaf or hashish, growers avoid the authorities by using mail-order and exchanging information via the Internet.

Young workers harvest cannabis plants in a fertile valley in Lebanon. Cannabis is an important crop in many poor countries, even though it is illegal.

Some home growers have used intensive farming techniques to develop new strains of cannabis such as skunk. Like farmers growing wheat, potatoes or other crops, they are trying to develop plants that will grow quickly and produce a large harvest. The other aim for cannabis growers is to find strains that are stronger – in other words, strains that contain a higher concentration of THC, the active ingredient of cannabis.

All this has become big business, with many growers planting cannabis in large outdoor plots or cultivating it on a large scale indoors, using special lamps to create hothouse conditions that are ideal for growing. Some growers sell seeds for strains that contain more than double the amount of THC that cannabis typically had 20 years ago. In 2005, some American drug officials were warning of new strains that contained up to 10 times more THC compared to the cannabis of the 1970s and 1980s, when many adults first tried it.

Cannabis growing in intensive conditions in Stockholm, Sweden.

CANNABIS SLANG

There are hundreds of slang terms to describe cannabis, its effects, how it is taken and much more. These terms often fade from use, only to replaced by others. Here are some current terms:

Baked: *high on cannabis.*
Blaze: *to smoke cannabis.*
Dagga: *a South African term for cannabis.*
Deal: *to sell cannabis.*
Dope: *slang for cannabis.*
Eighth: *a common amount of cannabis sold (one-eighth of an ounce).*
Ganja: *originally a Hindi term for cannabis.*
Herb: *slang for cannabis.*
Joint: *a hand-rolled cannabis cigarette (sometimes mixed with tobacco).*
Marijuana: *a term for cannabis.*
Munchies: *the feeling of hunger when someone is high.*
Reefer: *slang for a joint.*
Roach: *a cardboard filter used in a joint.*
Skins: *cigarette papers used to roll joints.*
Skunk: *a wide-ranging term for powerful cannabis. It describes either a strain of the cannabis plant high in THC or the flowering tops of some cannabis plants.*
Stoned: *high on cannabis.*
Toke up: *to smoke cannabis.*
Wasted: *high on cannabis.*

People find all sort of reasons to take substances which change the way they feel or behave. They might be insecure, unhappy, worried or simply curious. They might just want to have a good time. These are all reasons why people take cannabis, just as they might choose alcohol or cocaine or ecstasy. Many people find that getting high and being high is fun. It offers a chance to see things differently and sometimes to share this experience with others.

Many young people turn to cannabis as a way of staying close to friends who use the drug.

Peer pressure

But people who smoke cannabis know it is illegal. Even if they believe it is harmless, they know they run the risk of being caught. People who say "it's a free country" or "no-one is forcing you to smoke a joint" ignore a powerful reason why many people begin taking cannabis.

Most people first become exposed to cannabis in their teens, an age when it is very important to feel cool or part of a group. If one or more members of a group begin smoking cannabis, then others often feel the need to follow. Otherwise, they fear they will seem cowardly or uncool. Peer pressure is the reason many people begin taking the drug.

The festival spirit

Many people describe being high as feeling mellow – a sort of smiling good mood where nothing seems to bother them. Troubles seem to fade away as people think more about enjoying what is happening around them. The mellow feeling is heightened among a group of friends, or even with strangers who have come together for a party or some other gathering.

Pop festivals, such as those at Glastonbury and Reading in the UK, or Australia's annual Falls Festival, have become an ideal place for sharing cannabis. People pass joints to each other through the crowd and share in a group feeling of warmth and friendliness. Stall-holders provide festival-goers with a range of snacks and blow-out meals because they know that people who are high need to eat. The feeling of being at a festival – often described as being a buzz in itself – can be another type of peer pressure. Many festival-goers feel they are somehow losing out on the full experience if they don't join the others and smoke some joints.

Cannabis, like alcohol, can cause people to lose their inhibitions (social fears and embarrassment) when they are in a large crowd.

Here are some answers given by five teenagers from Bath, who were asked why they occasionally smoked cannabis.

● *To relax.*

● *To forget problems related to school or friends.*

● *Because it might be dangerous.*

● *Because many of their friends take it.*

● *To help them get to sleep.*

● *Because it is cheaper than alcohol.*

● *Because they are curious.*

● *To relieve boredom.*

● *Because it is around (friends or older brothers and sisters have it).*

● *To rebel (their parents don't want them to take it).*

● *To have a bit of a laugh.*

DISCOVERING SHAKESPEARE

Below Sarah, a university student, tells how she first took cannabis at school in London.

"It was the end of Year 10 and I was part of a school group that went to an open-air production of Midsummer Night's Dream in Regent's Park. We had been studying it in English and our teacher was saying that it was really funny if you saw it (we found that hard to believe).

"Once we had found a spot for our picnic blankets some of us went off to the loo. Behind some bushes near the loo, one of my friends then lit up a hand-rolled cigarette. She took a couple drags then passed it on to the girl next to her. She passed it to me. I wasn't stupid and I figured what it was from the smell and the way the girls kept looking over their shoulders to see whether anyone was watching.

"I decided to give it a go. I don't smoke, so when I took a puff I coughed really loudly. The girls got shirty, saying I was wasting it and attracting attention. But I tried another puff and held that one in. The joint made the rounds two or three more times, with me getting more experienced each time.

"We went back to the group just as the play was starting. I started to feel high for the first time. I got a bit distracted looking at the branches of the trees and I was convinced I could hear every leaf rustling when there was a breeze. Then I started watching the play. I couldn't believe how funny it was. My friends and I started laughing in the first scene and kept it up to the end. Our teacher must have sussed what was up, judging by her expression, but because we seemed to be enjoying it, she didn't let on.

"I've smoked it quite a few times since then, but less now that I'm at college. Part of me still finds it fun. Another part, though, thinks that if you find everything funny then you start to lose your judgement about what really is funny. And maybe that's not so good."

Howard Marks served seven years in an American prison for drug-dealing crimes but still campaigns for legalizing cannabis.

SEARCHING QUESTION

Sarah, the university student interviewed above, seems to be outgrowing cannabis; she now believes the reason she found so many things funny or clever were because the drug tricked her into thinking they were. Do you think she would have believed anyone who told her that before she smoked it?

FACT

In 2001, Australia's Commonwealth Department of Health and Aged Care, published figures which showed that:

● 39 per cent of Australians report that they've used cannabis at some point in their lives. Around two-thirds of 18–25 year-olds say they've tried it.

● About 20 per cent of young men use cannabis weekly or more often.

In 2004, the European Monitoring Centre for Drugs and Drug Addiction found that two in five 15-year-olds in the UK had tried cannabis – more than in any other European country. About one in ten in the same age group had smoked cannabis more than 40 times in the previous year.

A man openly smokes a large cannabis joint during the Marijuana March for Freedom in the Canadian capital, Ottawa, in June 2004.

Cannabis affects different people in different ways. How a person feels after smoking or eating cannabis depends on many things, such as their mood beforehand, how strong the cannabis is and whether they also have another drug such as alcohol in their body. It takes only a few minutes for the THC to reach the brain if cannabis is smoked (an hour or more if it is eaten) and the high begins to wear off after a couple of hours. If a user takes more cannabis during this time the high is usually prolonged.

The sense of becoming high can be like the feeling when someone suddenly sees the image hidden in a 3-D picture, such as the one above.

Like a daydream

As the drug takes effect, users begin to experience some sights and sounds, such as music, more deeply. When they are high, or stoned, their ordinary thoughts slip away and they may concentrate on just one sight or sound – a melody, the feel of a leaf or some cloud patterns in the sky – rather like a daydream. Concentrating so hard sometimes makes it seem odd or terribly interesting – or just funny. It's a bit like the feeling you get when you repeat a name or a word over and over again until it becomes just a couple of funny, almost meaningless, sounds.

INSIDE THE BRAIN

The feelings people experience when they take cannabis are caused by chemical changes in the brain. The THC attaches itself to receptors in the brain's nerve cells and changes the way information is transmitted. Some parts of the brain have more receptors than others, particularly the mid-brain.

Receptors in areas of the mid-brain, such as the hippocampus, septal area and the cingulate cortex (shown below), seem to be greatly affected. These are the places we store memories and feel emotions.

THC can affect the way new information is stored in the brain's long-term memory. This might explain why stoned people seem so forgetful, sometimes losing track of what they are saying in the middle of a sentence. THC may also produce sudden and profound feelings that may make the user find things funny, sad or scary.

FACT

Researchers at Harvard University in the US report that the risk of having a heart attack is five times higher than usual in the hour after someone has smoked cannabis.

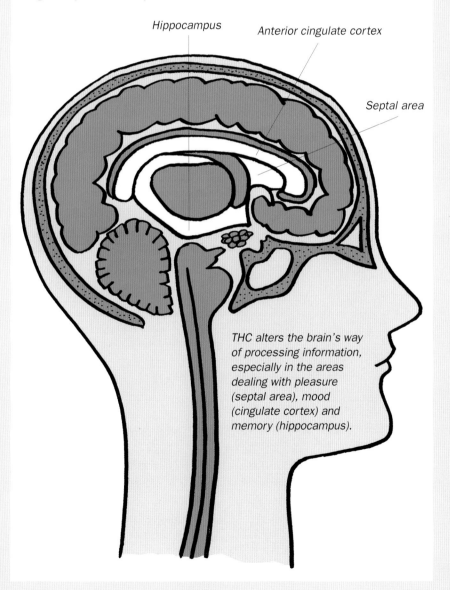

Hippocampus

Anterior cingulate cortex

Septal area

THC alters the brain's way of processing information, especially in the areas dealing with pleasure (septal area), mood (cingulate cortex) and memory (hippocampus).

Cannabis fuels the munchies – a boost in appetite that is a powerful urge to eat your favourite foods.

Losing track of time

People who smoke or eat cannabis also lose track of time. For example, they might look at a coin for five minutes, examining the shape of the letters, the feel of the metal, the details of the picture on it, and even the clink if they drop it on the floor. They may also lose their short-term memory – within a few minutes they could forget they have been looking at the coin!

The munchies

A common side-effect of taking cannabis is a boost to the appetite, usually referred to as the munchies. This can occur soon after taking the drug, but more often after about three hours, when the other effects of the drug have worn off. Scientists believe the THC in cannabis acts on a part of the brain that stimulates the appetite, leading to a powerful craving for food.

WHAT TO LOOK FOR

Cannabis affects people in different ways, and some people have very different experiences each time they take it. Below are some of the common effects; many of them are not pleasant.

● *Dry mouth.*

● *Red eyes.*

● *Faster heartbeat.*

● *Becoming really hungry (often called the munchies).*

● *Poor memory and concentration.*

● *Confused sense of time.*

● *Changed moods.*

Driving while high on cannabis is dangerous because the driver is less able to judge what is happening and may even become paranoid about being followed.

DEEP THOUGHTS

Gary, a Londoner in his 20s, remembers how he felt the first few times he took cannabis.

"My mates and I found ourselves looking at a fashion magazine that my sister had left in the sitting room. None of us would ever have opened this magazine, but it was the only thing there to look at. There we were, three lads staring at stitching and colours, talking about the shape of shoes – that sort of thing. One of us said that without the dope, we would never have been able to appreciate these things. He got a pencil and paper and started writing down some of our comments, 'cause we felt we'd be glad to look at them later. Somehow we managed to lose the piece of paper, but my mother found it a couple of days later. I took it and found that all that was written on it was 'even models have two feet'. Pretty deep, eh?"

Along a scary path

Cannabis users who concentrate hard and see things in a different way from normal might believe they are coming up with deep thoughts and important new ways of looking at life (see panel, left). But this concentration, while harmless or funny at times, can also take a person along a frightening path. They might begin thinking about things that had worried them before taking the cannabis – a homework project, whether a friend really likes them, or whether some passers-by have reported them to the police. This sort of intense worry can lead to a form of paranoia, which is a strong feeling that the world is against you.

This woman's badge shows that she supports the campaign to make cannabis legal.

People who take any mood-changing drug over a long period of time will be affected by changes to their health. The effects differ from person to person. Some people can carry on with their lives, feeling no ill-effects. For others, the long-term effects can be troubling – physically, psychologically and socially.

Physical effects

People who smoke cannabis are likely to experience some of the problems linked to tobacco smoking. Although most regular cannabis users don't smoke nearly as many joints as tobacco smokers do cigarettes, joints are more harmful. Scientists calculate that some of the cancer-causing ingredients of a cigarette, especially tar, are highly concentrated in joints. Smoke, whether from tobacco or cannabis, irritates breathing passages and lungs, causing wheezing and coughing.

Prolonged cannabis use can lead to more serious breathing illnesses, such as bronchitis, pneumonia and even lung cancer. Scientific studies of animals show that THC harms the body's immune system, so people are more likely to catch colds and other infections. Studies in the US support this: because of health problems, regular cannabis smokers missed more days of school and work than non-smokers.

" Cannabis contains more than 400 chemicals, including most of the harmful substances found in tobacco smoke. Smoking one marijuana cigarette deposits about four times more tar into the lungs than a filtered tobacco cigarette. "

Greater Dallas (Texas) Council on Alcohol and Drug Abuse.

➡

A doctor looks at an X-ray of a lung. A cannabis joint is far more harmful to the lungs than a cigarette.

Jayne (not her real name) was interviewed on the ABC Radio National programme All in the Mind in Australia in March 2002. She had enjoyed an occasional joint during her teens, but at 19 smoked more often, sometimes as much as once an hour. She began to have strange and unpleasant thoughts, even when she hadn't had any cannabis.

"I thought I would die in my sleep. I thought that if I went to sleep, the people in my household would all die. So I was up, literally, [for] days, not wanting to sleep... I was up on a farm thinking that the dogs were looking at me directly. So I thought I was a dog like them, and that was extremely scary... I really thought these things were happening to me."

Psychologists describe Jayne's state of mind as psychosis because she has hallucinations (she sees or hears things that are not there) or has delusions (she believes things that are not true).

The Early Psychosis Prevention and Intervention Centre in Melbourne successfully treated Jayne. It is a specialist service for people aged between 15 and 30 – the peak age range for both using cannabis and the first signs of psychosis.

Mental muddles

Over the past 30 years or so, as cannabis use has become more widespread, people have noticed that some regular cannabis users seem to be vague and uninterested in things. They lose interest in trying out new activities, or in pushing themselves at school or at work. It's as if they are in a mental muddle and saying "Who cares?".

Psychologists have a term to describe this type of behaviour – amotivational syndrome. People need to be motivated, to have a determination that drives them to do their best. One danger of cannabis is that many users lose this inner drive and seem to prefer escaping from reality. This is especially dangerous for young people, who need qualifications in order to find interesting and satisfying jobs in later life.

Medical students learn about the long-term health effects of cannabis during their years of training to become doctors.

Chilling out is a novelty at first but it can become the main activity of people who use cannabis over a long period.

No-one knows what causes this loss of drive, but it might be linked to the action of THC on the brain's ability to process information. Other psychological effects of long-term cannabis use are more serious and frightening, and may cause deeper trouble, such as schizophrenia or even psychosis.

Research into the psychological effects of cannabis can be confusing. It is hard to be sure that cannabis directly causes deep psychological problems, but many people believe there is a link. In October 2005, Dr Thomas Stuttaford wrote in *The Times* that, "A person who suffers a psychotic breakdown after cannabis, had he not smoked it, might well have journeyed happily through life being no more than mildly eccentric."

❝ It just f*s with your head. I had to sleep with a knife under my bed 'cos I used to think people were going to come in and bash me during the night or something. Just for me mull (cannabis) or something, yeah. ❞**

Danni, 17, interviewed on *Messing With Heads*, shown on ABC (Australia) TV, 7 March 2005.

SEARCHING QUESTION
Some supporters of cannabis suggest that users who develop psychosis might have become that way even without taking cannabis. Opponents say that might be true, but that 'might' is the important word, and even a small risk is not worth taking. What do you think?

Hooked on smoke?

For many users, taking cannabis becomes part of a routine when they meet other people. What starts out as an escape can turn into a habit.

One of the big questions surrounding cannabis – and any drug, whether legal or illegal – is whether it is habit-forming. Are people driven to take it more and more often, even if they know they shouldn't? To answer this we need to understand the nature of dependence.

Experts talk about two types of drug dependence: physical dependence and psychological dependence. Either (or both) of these can develop after a person takes a drug regularly and develops a habit. And either (or both) can exert a powerful hold on people.

Heroin and alcohol are good examples of drugs that lead to physical dependence: the body becomes so accustomed to having the drug that

↑

Long-term users of cannabis become experts at rolling joints wherever they happen to be.

it depends on having it. When the drug is withdrawn (taken away), the person has a powerful and unpleasant experience known as withdrawal. Cannabis can produce a mild type of withdrawal. Another feature of physical dependence is the need to take more of the drug in order to reach the same high. This is sometimes the case with cannabis, but not nearly as much as heroin.

Psychological dependence describes a person's need to use a drug just to feel normal. Cannabis does not seem to cause this feeling in the way that other drugs, such as alcohol or tobacco, do. However, it can make people want to take it again and again. Many regular users feel cannabis is an important part of their daily lives and is the only way they can relax, unwind, deal with unhappiness or simply deal with everyday events. Also, some of the effects that cannabis produces – especially making boring things seem funny or interesting – make some people become irritable when they are not high.

PART OF MY LIFE

Sam (not his real name) has been a regular cannabis user for 30 years. He was studying to be a doctor in the US, but was expelled for smoking cannabis instead of going to lectures. He now works as a handyman.

"I managed to study hard at school and at college, even though I was smoking pretty regularly – three or four times a week. It kind of got on top of me after a while, as if something was going to have to go.

"I started skipping classes at college, but I think some of the instructors saw me looking pretty red-eyed and out of it when I should have been in classes.

"It sucked being dumped by the university, especially when my friends were getting qualifications. I kept on smoking though, maybe to help me forget the whole experience. It seemed at that point that the dope had become part of my life. And I guess it's stayed that way since. I keep thinking of new things to do, but in the end it just seems easier to light up and turn off for a while."

Regular cannabis users often have bloodshot (red) eyes, because THC increases the flow of blood into the capillaries in the eyes.

DECIDING FOR THEMSELVES

Many drug counsellors believe that users have to decide for themselves whether or not they are dependent on cannabis. People are more likely to change their behaviour if they have decided something for themselves. Users might be asked to draw up two lists: What I like about cannabis and What I don't like about cannabis. Then they are asked to check which list is longer. Doing this regularly helps some people to realize they have become dependent on cannabis and to sort their dependence themselves.

Typical lists might include the following:

WHAT I LIKE ABOUT CANNABIS

● It makes me feel mellow.

● Dull things are more interesting and maybe even funny.

● It's fun to take with friends.

● Cannabis doesn't make people violent or aggressive like alcohol does.

● It seems to be less harmful than most drugs, and is certainly less harmful than alcohol or tobacco.

WHAT I DON'T LIKE ABOUT CANNABIS

● I seem to sit around doing nothing a lot.

● I spend too much money on cannabis.

● It's hard to tell whether things really are that funny if everything seems funny when you're stoned.

● I don't seem to have so many plans for the future.

● My circle of friends has got smaller and only seems to include others who smoke a lot of cannabis.

SEARCHING QUESTION

Sam (see panel on page 30) has been smoking cannabis for many years. At what point in his life do you think he became dependent on it? Do you think he realized it at the time, and do you think he considers himself dependent on it now?

Border Patrol agents question a group of illegal immigrants trying to cross into the US from Mexico. Much US cannabis comes from Mexico and other countries in Latin America, often transported by poor migrants.

Youth is a time of growing and maturing, mentally as well as physically. Most adults who are blown off course for a while because of cannabis have finished their education or achieved basic qualifications which will help them find jobs. They can put their drug use behind them and get on with their lives.

Young people often lose that choice if they have been distracted from learning because of their use of cannabis. Finding the normal world boring and uninteresting is dangerous if that world involves preparing for exams that could shape the rest of a person's life. Without qualifications, a young person can miss out on the career of their choice – or on changing from one career to another in later life.

More at stake

Young people face more immediate problems when they take cannabis. Adults usually know what they are taking, either because they have a cannabis supplier they trust or because they grow it themselves. Young people who might not even know what cannabis looks like have to trust whoever sells it to them. It might be incredibly strong or it might be mixed with other drugs. Either way, the results could be terrifying.

What cannabis does to long-term memory is another big problem. People who smoke it may risk permanently harming their memory and their ability to learn.

The legal complications surrounding cannabis are also more serious for young people. If they are caught and get a police record related to cannabis, young people – with little or no work experience – will find it hard to be accepted for a job.

" I have seen very smart young men degenerate into a complete mess during a psychotic episode triggered (by) smoking skunk. "

Abu Al Rahman, London Region Officer of the Federation of Black and Asian Drug and Alcohol Workers.

" We've got two-thirds of young people using it now. They're using forms of the drug... where the THC content, for example, is often unknown. And they're using it in ways that are very risky and we're not doing a good job of educating [them] about the risks. "

Professor Wayne Hall,
Queensland University, Australia.

Using cannabis regularly makes it harder to play sports because it affects the body's ability to judge distance and movement.

SEARCHING QUESTION

Many reports and users' accounts say that taking cannabis over long periods of time plays tricks with and even damages people's memory. Can you think of reasons why such a result would be even more worrying for a young person than for an adult?

Many of life's big debates have enough uncertainty to make it hard to come up with an easy answer. The issue of cannabis, especially whether or not it should be made legal, is an ethical debate that has divided people for decades. Each side seems to be stuck in their view and is unwilling to judge the other side's argument fairly.

The argument against

Some people believe that any drug which changes the way people behave is dangerous and should be made illegal. In their view, cannabis poses many risks, including some that may be unknown. They say that legalizing cannabis and making it easier to buy would lead to all sorts of problems, both for the people who take it and for society. According to this argument, cannabis users would make poor parents, teachers and leaders for the future because of their bored attitude and lack of motivation.

Canadians campaigning to legalize cannabis have replaced the maple leaf on their national flag with a cannabis-leaf emblem.

> **Drugs to me is cocaine, heroin. Herb (cannabis) is the healing of the nation.**
>
> Paul David, a Rastafarian living in New York, 1998.

FREEDOM OF RELIGION

Some religious groups use cannabis in their ceremonies. Rastafarians, for example, believe cannabis is holy and an essential part of worship. It is a sacrament, like the bread and wine that Christians take in Communion. Rastafarians in Jamaica and other countries have argued that laws guaranteeing freedom of religion should allow them to use cannabis.

Americans in favour of such an approach point out that, although all alcoholic drinks were illegal in the US between 1919 and 1933, Christian churches were still allowed to use wine in their worship.

Some people say that governments could earn vast amounts of money from tax if cannabis were sold legally in the same way as cigarettes.

> **" I just want to know why I can't grow it in the privacy of my own home and smoke it in the privacy of my own home. I don't drink alcohol, I just ask if I can take cannabis for my multiple sclerosis. That's all I ask. Please. "**

Barry Clark, speaking at a debate entitled *Cannabis: Should it be decriminalized?* in London, 11 December 1997.

The argument for

Other people take a very different view. They argue that cannabis does not lead to violence and broken families in the way alcohol can. Despite the evidence (see pages 24–27) they believe that, unlike tobacco, cannabis does not lead to medical complications. In short, they say cannabis does not damage its users permanently and is a harmless way of relaxing.

They say legalizing cannabis would remove the problem of not knowing exactly what is being sold. Government inspections could guarantee the quality of the cannabis sold, just as they guarantee other legal products, such as shampoo and vitamins. In addition, cannabis sold legally could be taxed, so governments could earn money in the process. As a result, criminals who deal in cannabis would probably go out of business.

Medical help

Supporters of legalization often quote its medical benefits. Cannabis has been used medically for centuries, mainly to relieve pain. In most countries, though, the drug remains illegal because governments have believed that legalizing cannabis for medical reasons would weaken cannabis laws generally.

Since the 1970s, though, many medical experts have come to support legalizing cannabis for some specific treatments. Evidence is mounting that THC, the active ingredient in cannabis, has real benefits in treating the eye condition glaucoma and the nerve disease multiple sclerosis (MS).

Glaucoma is a leading cause of blindness in many countries. Studies have shown that people with glaucoma felt less pressure (and pain) in their eyes after taking cannabis.

Multiple sclerosis affects people's nervous systems, causing pain and making movements difficult to control. Some people with MS have reported pain relief and easier movement after taking cannabis. Doctors cannot agree whether these improvements are because of cannabis and, if they are, whether the drug could fully treat MS over a longer period.

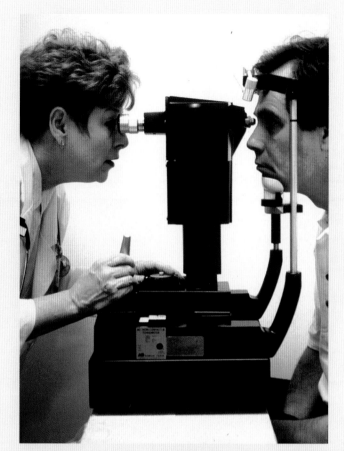

An eye specialist examines the eyes of a person with glaucoma. Some evidence suggests that cannabis can help treat this disease.

> **" Remember though that cigarettes are not new and novel. They've been abused for centuries. If the same thing were to happen with marijuana (cannabis) because of new freedoms, I'd be frightened. To put it mildly. I've seen what happens to people who think they know moderation. It's not at all pleasant. "**

A post by balamm (blogger's name) on a filesharingtalk.com web site in response to the question "Will drugs become legal?"

SEARCHING QUESTION

Imagine you were a politician who had just been elected to represent your country's government. Would you consider changing the laws on cannabis an important issue? Would you make it legal for everyone, or only in certain medical cases such as sufferers of multiple sclerosis and glaucoma?

A number of people in many countries believe cannabis is harmless and should be made legal (see pages 34–37). Most people, though, believe either that cannabis is dangerous or that we don't know enough yet to be sure it is safe. This majority view explains why the drug remains illegal, although the laws controlling cannabis (and how they are enforced) are constantly being studied and sometimes changed.

Tough measures

Many schools in the US operate a zero-tolerance approach to cannabis and other drugs. Under this system, anyone found with cannabis in (or sometimes even near) a school is automatically expelled with no questions asked. This system has its opponents, but supporters say pupils perform better and their education benefits as a result.

Other schools take a similar approach by testing students randomly for drugs. Faversham School in Kent was the first school in the UK to adopt this approach, beginning in January 2004. Twenty pupils, chosen at random, are tested at the secondary school each week. The school contacts the parents of anyone testing positive (showing traces of drugs), but only those who are known to be selling drugs are expelled.

In August 2005, Faversham School published the results of the first GCSE exams taken under a full year of the new system. The results were better than the year before: 40 per cent achieved five good GCSE passes compared with 26 per cent in 2004. Head teacher Peter Walker believes the random drug testing played a part in this improvement by helping pupils concentrate on their studies: "It has had an effect on contributions in the classroom and on behaviour – with far less disruption and that sort of thing."

The financial costs of policing cannabis amount to at least £50 million a year (including sentencing costs), and absorb the equivalent of 500 full-time police officers.

From a 2002 report by the Joseph Rowntree Foundation (a social charity), studying the cost of enforcing UK cannabis laws before the drug was reclassified.

Some countries, such as the UK (see page 41), have cannabis laws that apply nationally. Others, such as Australia and the US, leave much of the law-making (and enforcing) to state or regional governments. So the punishments for possessing cannabis can vary a great deal in one country. For example, in Australia in 2005 the maximum punishment for possessing 100 grams of cannabis ranged from A$150 (in South Australia) to 15 years' imprisonment (in Queensland).

The American position is even more complicated. In mid-2005, 10 states had laws allowing the use of cannabis for medical purposes. But the US federal (national) laws do not allow this use of cannabis. The result is likely to be a lengthy battle in the courts to decide whether the states are free to enforce their own laws. In the meantime, millions of Americans remain confused about the legal position of cannabis.

New approaches

Many people who believe cannabis should remain illegal agree that using it is less serious than other illegal activities – robbery and assault, for example. They believe that the police could serve the public better by concentrating on these more serious crimes (and more serious drugs, such as heroin and cocaine) rather than using time and money to track down every cannabis user.

Some countries, especially the Netherlands, have long held this view and have decriminalized cannabis. It is still technically illegal to use cannabis,

A Cuban soldier stands guard over a large amount of cannabis that was confiscated from Jamaican drug dealers. The drug will soon be transported to a secure site and burned.

although the police do not arrest anyone with less than 30 grams of the drug. The Dutch police also allow certain coffee shops to sell up to 5 grams of cannabis to people over the age of 18. Local or regional police forces operate similar policies in other parts of the world, such as Vancouver in Canada and Malaga in southern Spain.

Some coffee shops in the Dutch city of Amsterdam are allowed to sell small amounts of cannabis to customers who can only smoke inside the shop.

Changing the category

In the UK, the government classifies (puts in categories) a drug depending on how harmful they believe it to be. Category (or Class) A drugs, such as heroin, cocaine and LSD, are the most dangerous and the penalties for selling and possessing them are the most severe.

In 2004, the UK changed the category of cannabis from B to C. The only real change is that the maximum penalty for possessing cannabis is reduced from five years in jail to two. First-time offenders under the age of 18 are taken to a police station for a formal warning in the presence of their parents or guardians. Later offences can still lead to a conviction in the courts, which can prevent people from visiting some countries, including Australia and the US.

Taking cannabis can be a confusing and frightening experience and the people you would normally turn to, such as close friends and family members, might not be able to help. Perhaps they think it is no big deal or perhaps you have lost touch with your own family as well as older friends who don't smoke cannabis.

Other sources of help

Perhaps you are embarrassed to talk about using cannabis to family members or other people you know. Your school or local library will have books and leaflets giving addresses and email information for groups that specialize in providing advice and guidance.

Websites are also worth looking at. For example, Talk to Frank is a UK site with all sorts of information and links, while Reach Out provides a similar service in Australia. Other websites are run by international cannabis-awareness organizations that often have branches near you. Marijuana Anonymous, for example, uses traditions of trust and co-operation to help people overcome their heavy use of cannabis. Just as importantly, it has information to help young people deal with heavy cannabis use by other family members.

The best support for young people can come from within the family, if members are prepared to discuss cannabis and other difficult subjects freely.

Professional help

Medical professionals who have experience with alcohol and drug dependence can help people who have serious problems with cannabis. Private cannabis clinics are becoming more common in many countries, and some governments are building their own.

In 2003, the first of four cannabis clinics to be built by the Australian government opened in Parramatta, in southern Sydney. It has already proved to be a success. More than half the people treated at the clinic have stopped using cannabis altogether (some had been spending A$300 a week on cannabis); most of the others had cut down considerably.

" This is part of a comprehensive response the government's been taking to the emerging problem of links between cannabis use and cannabis overuse and various health, psychiatric and social problems affecting young people. "

Australian Special Minister of State John Della Bosca speaking about the Parramatta cannabis clinic in Sydney, 2003.

Prince Harry went to Featherstone Lodge, a London drug-treatment centre, for a day in 2001 after his father learned he had smoked cannabis.

FEATHERSTONE LODGE

administered given by a doctor or nurse

amotivational syndrome a mental condition in which a person loses interest in important things in life

amphetamines illegal drugs that work on the nervous system to lift a person's mood

bronchitis painful irritation of the breathing passages

cash crop a plant grown because of the money it can fetch when harvested

cocaine a drug used in medicine as a painkiller and illegally as a way of boosting mood and confidence

dealers people who sell illegal drugs

depression a mental condition in which a person feels sad and unable to perform ordinary tasks

ecstasy an illegal drug that lifts a user's mood for several hours

emotions strong feelings such as excitement and sadness

expelled banned from school permanently

First World War a global conflict, lasting from 1914 to 1918, involving many countries mainly in Europe

glaucoma an eye illness caused by increased pressure on the eyeball, sometimes leading to blindness

Hindi one of the main languages spoken in India

majority more than half of a group

malaria a disease causing chills and fevers, spread when mosquitoes bite humans

menstrual describing the monthly cycle of women of childbearing age. During the cycle an unfertilized egg is shed with the womb lining. This can cause painful cramps called period pains.

moderation not doing something too much

multiple sclerosis a disease resulting from damage to the brain or nervous system, causing pain and loss of balance

opium an illegal drug that dulls the senses and sends people to sleep

paranoia the belief (because of a mental condition) that the outside world is hostile

peer pressure persuasion from peers to do something in order to remain part of the group

peers people of a similar age or social group

pneumonia a disease of the lungs leading to coughing, fever and difficulty in breathing

psychosis a mental condition that leads a person to lose contact with reality

Rastafarian a member of a religious group which originated in Jamaica and which considers cannabis to be a holy plant

reclassified put in a different legal category

recreationally (in the case of drugs) taken for pleasure rather than for a medical reason

resin a sticky substance that comes from the sap of a plant

Suggested reading

rheumatism the name given to several medical conditions that lead to swelling and stiffness of muscles and joints

sacrament a religious act that is a symbol of someone's beliefs

schizophrenia a severe psychosis that distorts someone's view of the real world

serrated having notches around the edges

strain a variety of a plant

tax a charge made by a government on income or on the sale of things

tincture a drug mixed with alcohol so that it can be drunk

withdrawal physical and psychological changes in a person who has stopped taking a substance after developing a dependence on it

Books

Drug Abuse? (Viewpoints series) E. Haughton. (Franklin Watts, 2004)

The Score: Facts About Drugs (Health Education Authority, 1998)

Buzzed: The Straight Facts About the Most Used Drugs from Alcohol to Ecstasy C. Kuhn. (Norton, 2003)

Drugs: the Truth (Teenage Health Freak) A. Macfarlane and A. McPherson. (Oxford University Press, 2003)

Drugs A. Naik. (Hodder Children's Books, 1997)

Cannabis A. Royston. (Heinemann, 2001)

What Do You Know About Drugs? P. Sanders and N. Myers. (Franklin Watts, 2000)

Websites

ABC Online (Australia)
www.abc.net.au
The website for the ABC radio and television network has a powerful search engine to link users to stories and downloads about cannabis and other drug issues.

D-World (UK)
www.drugscope.org.uk/wip/24/
A special section of the informative DrugScope site aimed at 11–14 year-olds.

KIDS HELP LINE (Australia)
www.kidshelp.com.au
A phone (freecall 1800 55 1800) and web-based counselling service for 5–18 year-olds.

Reach Out (Australia)
www.reachout.com.au/home.asp
Provides informative and downloadable fact sheets about cannabis and other drugs. Deals with a range of emotional issues and inspirational stories.

Talk to Frank (UK)
www.talktofrank.com/
Provides downloadable drug information for 11–14 year-olds. Helps to explain myths and offers sound advice about cannabis and other drugs.

Urge (New Zealand)
www.whakamanawa.org.nz
Provides details about cannabis and other drugs, plus other important teen issues.

Where's Your Head At? (Australia)
www.drugs.health.gov.au/youth/
Provides detailed drug information, stories, legal advice and competitions.

Index